MAGIC CASTLE READERS®

What Can We Play Today?

A book about community helpers

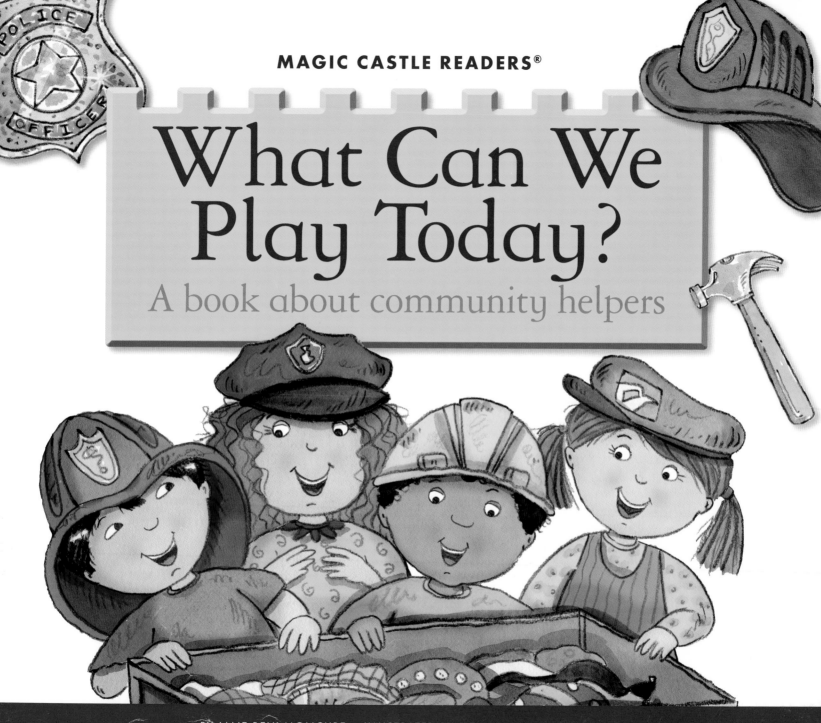

BY JANE BELK MONCURE • ILLUSTRATED BY MERNIE GALLAGHER-COLE

The Child's World

Published by The Child's World®
1980 Lookout Drive • Mankato, MN 56003-1705
800-599-READ • www.childsworld.com

Acknowledgments
The Child's World®: Mary Berendes, Publishing Director
The Design Lab: Design
Jody Jensen Shaffer: Editing

ISBN 9781623235871
LCCN 2013931349

Printed in the United States of America
Mankato, MN
July 2013
PA02177

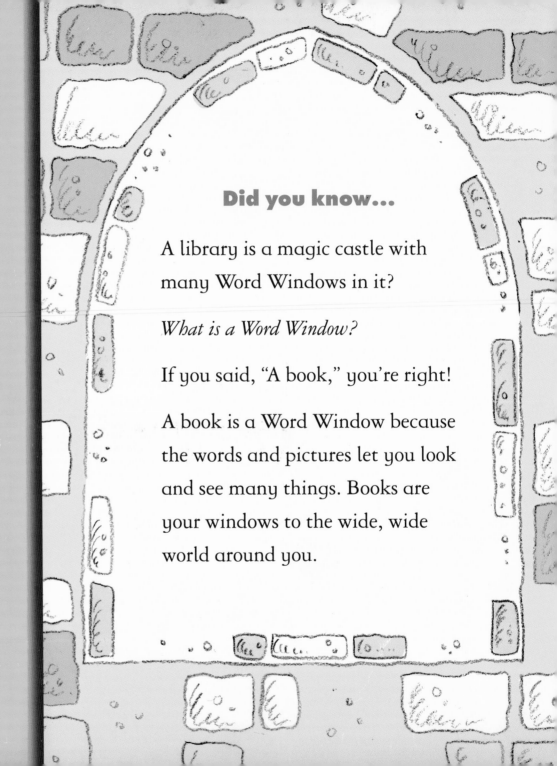

Did you know...

A library is a magic castle with many Word Windows in it?

What is a Word Window?

If you said, "A book," you're right!

A book is a Word Window because the words and pictures let you look and see many things. Books are your windows to the wide, wide world around you.

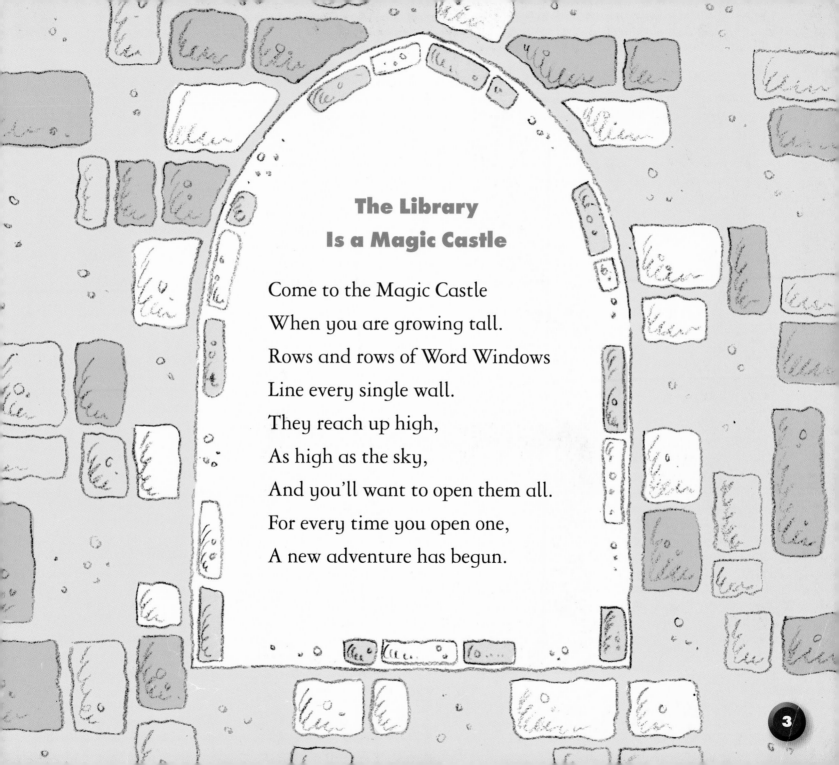

The Library Is a Magic Castle

Come to the Magic Castle
When you are growing tall.
Rows and rows of Word Windows
Line every single wall.
They reach up high,
As high as the sky,
And you'll want to open them all.
For every time you open one,
A new adventure has begun.

Jack opened a Word Window.
Here is what he read:

What can we play today?
We can play dress-up.

Look in the Dress-up box.
What do you see?

Can you guess who we will be?

We will be firefighters, that's who.
What do firefighters do?

They put out fires. That's what they do.

Get the ladder. Get the hose.
Swish! Out the fire goes.

Firefighters fight all kinds of fires.

Look in the box again. What do you see?
Can you guess who we will be?

Police officers, that's who.
What do police officers do?

They help keep us safe wherever we go.

Police officers help us know
when to stop and when to go.

And when someone is in trouble,
police officers come on the double.

Look in the box again. What do you see?
Can you guess who we will be?

A doctor and a nurse, that's who.
What do doctors and nurses do?

They take care of sick people.
That's what they do.

Doctors and nurses help people stay well and happy every day.

Look in the box again. What do you see?
Can you guess who we will be?

Fix-it people, that's who.
What do fix-it people do?

They fix things. That's what they do.

They fix a roof, a car, or a broken door.

They fix a broken pipe under a floor.

Look in the box again. What do you see?
Can you guess who we will be?

Mail carriers, that's who.
What do mail carriers do?

They carry letters, postcards, and packages, too.

They carry mail from the post office right to you.

Before we put all these things away, tell us:
who will YOU be today?

Jack closed the Word Window.

Questions and Activities

(Write your answers on a sheet of paper.)

1. Name two things you learned about community helpers. What else would you like to know?

2. Did this story have any words you don't know? How can you find out what they mean?

3. What does it mean when the book says police officers come "on the double"? How can you tell what it means?

4. Page 14 tells about police officers.
   Page 19 tells about doctors and nurses.
   How are these two jobs similar?
   What is different about these jobs?

5. Tell this story to a friend. Take only two minutes. Which parts did you share?